Darvellina's
Special Saint

Written by

Harvey Rosenberg

Illustrated by

Carlos Brito

Darvellina's Special Saint

Darvellina's Special Saint is a story of an unhappy angel
who becomes human so she can return to her eternal Home.

Thanks to the following who edited,
commented on, lovingly critiqued and/or reviewed
Darvellina's Special Saint:
John & Natasha Downing, Sharon & Richard Malarich,
Bob Pearsall, Carol Thompson and Gloria Simmonds.

Special thanks to Carlos Brito whose illustrations sparkle and
jump off the pages right into your heart.
His illustrations are simple and innocent,
full of vibrant colors that make you smile with joy.

ISBN-13: 978-0-9822824-5-8
©2014

All Rights Reserved

No part of this book may be reproducedin any form by electronic or mechanical
means including photocopying, recording or information storage and
retrieval without permission in writing from the
publisher and copyright owner, except by a reviewer,
who may quotebrief passages in connection with a review. Thank you.

Published by
Go Jolly Books
www.gojollybooks.com
74 Gem Ln
Sandpoint, ID 83864

FIRST EDITION, GO JOLLY BOOKS, First Printing 2014
10 9 8 7 6 5 4 3 2 1 Printed in the U.S.A.

Darvellina's
Special Saint

Dedicated to seekers of truth of all ages
whose hearts search for unconditional love that only Masters,
Perfect Living Masters and Saints
can offer humans, who all have at least one thing in common:
our hearts yearn for more love.

Once upon a time in a region known as the astral plane, there lived a joyous 8 year-old angel with long curly hair named Darvellina.

Her job was to help suffering children be happy.

From early morning to late afternoon, she worked with five other angels:

Bob, the angel of Gratitude, whose job it was to fill a child's heart with thankfulness for all she had to be grateful for, beginning with the gift of the human body.

Melinda, the angel of Forgiveness, whose job it was to help a child forgive anyone who inflicted pain upon her. Melinda's job was the most difficult, because forgiving others was so hard to do.

Kathryn, the angel of Humor, whose job it was to give a child stories that made her laugh and forget her difficulties even if just for a moment.

Gloria, the angel of Beauty, whose job it was to plant seeds of art within each child's heart, so the child herself could beautify the world in whatever artistic form chose her.

James, the angel of Love, whose job it was to teach a child that whenever she was confused, the surest way to feel better was to ask herself, "What would love do now?" and patiently await the answer.

These angels sent Darvellina to all parts of the galaxy. When she reached her destination, she filled the heart of the chosen child with the gift from whichever angel had sent her.

The gift grew and grew as the child became a teenager, a young adult, then a woman who married and had her own child whose heart also took on the qualities of the gift.

The gift became a trusted "friend" to the suffering child, who no longer was burdened with that problem. The "friend" lived within each child's heart her entire life, and influenced all those whose path crossed hers.

Is it any wonder that Darvellina loved her job?

After work, she spent time with the five angels, which helped her to develop their qualities as well.

But angel years are much longer than Earth years. After what seemed an eternity, her heart yearned for her true Home, even though she lived a life most angels longed for.

Desperate for help, she prayed from the deepest recesses of her heart. An answer arrived almost immediately: meet with the five angels and a solution will make itself known.

Eagerly, she telepathically sent a message to Bob, Melinda, Kathryn, Gloria and James that she needed their wisdom for a personal (well, an angel) problem she faced.

Shortly, Darvellina found herself in Bob's Gratitude Café, with Bob himself serving her a thick, bubbly chocolate drink full of light, love and other nutrients her soul required.

Soon, the four other angels arrived and the Café was bursting with angel energy.

"Thank you all for coming so quickly," Darvellina said between sips of her bubbly chocolate. "I really need your support," she continued.

"How can we help you, my dear?" asked a concerned Melinda, the angel of Forgiveness.

"Have we been working you too hard?" questioned Gloria, the angel of Beauty.

"I know what the problem is," Kathryn, the angel of Humor exclaimed. "You haven't had a vacation in years and you're burned out from helping so many children."

"No, no, stop!" cried Darvellina, touched by her friends' concern.

"It's not that at all. It's that my heart hurts. My soul longs to be reunited with our Creator. I've had enough thrills and adventures, enough joys and sorrows, I just want to go Home," she stated emphatically.

"Well, what are you waiting for?" replied Gloria, known for her rapid-fire solutions to other's problems.

"You've met many Gurus, Masters, and possibly some Saints or Perfect Living Masters," Gloria continued.

"You know what you have to do," added Bob, the angel of Gratitude.

The five angels looked around at each other and began discussing the matter, while Darvellina sat silently.

Within moments, Darvellina found herself in a human body, which was much denser than her angel body, heading towards Earth, her job as an angel completed as she left the astral plane.

The angels decided that Darvellina would visit India, China, and North America to meet three Masters whom she had met during her work who could possibly help her to return Home.

Her first stop was India, and a 3-day meditation retreat with Sant Pyara. Disciples and initiates from around the world attended. Darvellina felt blessed to share love with other seekers of truth.

It was a rigorous retreat. Darvellina sat for meditation six to eight hours daily, sang bhajans, listened to satsang, and most importantly received loving darshan from Sant Pyara.

When she departed, Darvellina's heart overflowed from the unconditional love showered upon her from the humble, God-intoxicated Master, whom she thanked over and over for all of Her gifts.

Yet, Darvellina still felt drawn to pay homage to a second Master, Sant Bara Dila from China. So she set off for Dazu, the journey much longer as a human than as an angel.

Darvellina arrived at the ashram in Dazu, and was warmly greeted by Salibaba, a long time seeker of truth, who made her feel especially welcome.

The bell rang at 3am, which began a full day of meditation, singing, personal interviews, washing dishes as volunteer work and mountains of love directed to her heart.

Babaji, as He was affectionately called, generously, humorously, and humbly opened Darvellina's eyes to a new way of viewing life.

Though she left China with profound gratitude for this God-intoxicated soul, Darvellina had one more journey to make in her search for the One to take charge of her soul and take her Home.

She arrived in Paradise Valley, MT to get the Blessings of Percy Smith, a homegrown American Sant Mat Master and part of the spiritual revolution occurring throughout the United States of America.

Once again, Darvellina's heart was filled with unconditional love but as importantly, she discovered how to make the decision that would guide the rest of her life.

Percy Smith clearly stated that a seeker of truth knew whom her Master was by the invisible messages sent between Master and seeker, messages that uplifted the seeker's soul beyond description.

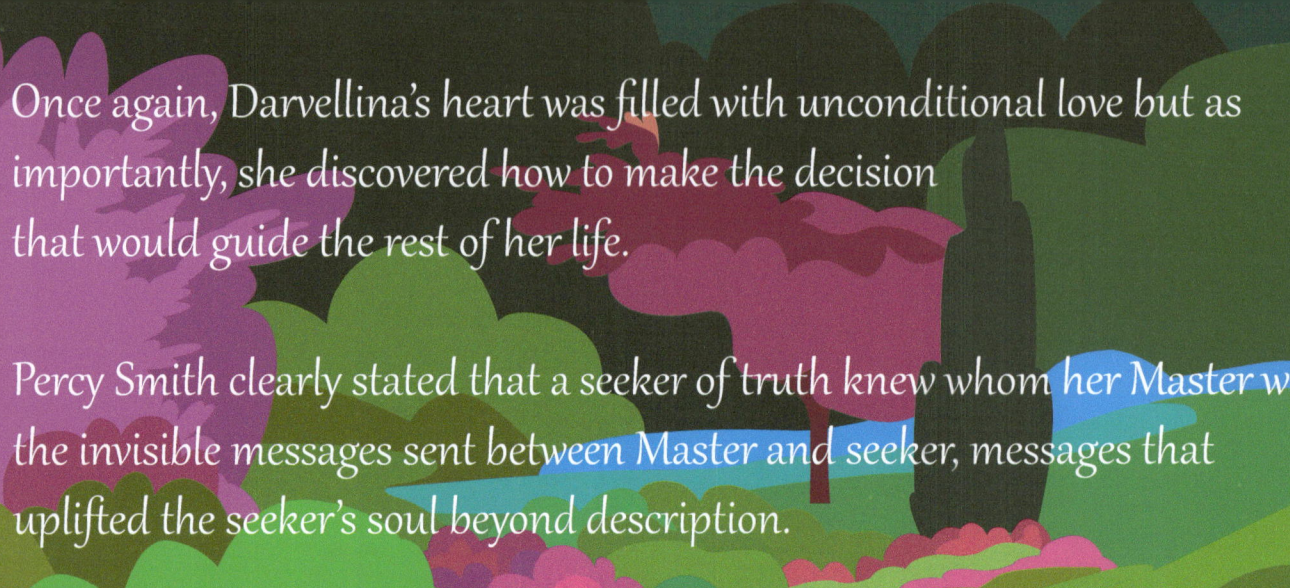

Darvellina's Master would strongly encourage her to satisfy her doubts and skepticism, to test the truth for herself, not simply to believe what she was told.

Darvellina's heart overflowed with joy, love and devotion after a week with Percy Smith. She felt a peaceful confidence, almost unshakeable faith, that the Creator, in time, would bring her Home.

As she settled into her new life on Earth, Darvellina knew that through prayer, intuition, inner guidance and coincidences she would discover her Master as she learned to go with the flow.

She would know Him by the amount of Love she felt for Him. The decision to follow a Master would be made through her heart and soul, so she felt no fear. Darvellina was happy for the first time in a very long while.

Someday, if you happen to pass through the USA,
and you see people dancing in the streets,
it just might be Darvellina and other seekers of truth,
moving to the Love in their hearts
for the Masters taking them Home.